MAMBAS
AMAZING SNAKES

Ted O'Hare

Rourke
Publishing LLC
Vero Beach, Florida 32964

www.rourkepublishing.com

PHOTO CREDITS: All photos © Lynn M. Stone except pp. 12, 15 © George Van Horn

Title page: *A West African green mamba's tongue darts out to sense the air.*

Editor: Frank Sloan

Cover and interior design by Nicola Stratford

Library of Congress Cataloging-in-Publication Data

O'Hare, Ted, 1961-
  Mambas / Ted O'Hare.
     p. cm. -- (Amazing snakes)
  Includes bibliographical references (p.   ).
  ISBN 1-59515-147-8 (hardcover)
  1. Mambas--Juvenile literature. I. Title. II. Series: O'Hare, Ted, 1961-   Amazing snakes.
  QL666.O64O42 2004
  597.96'4--dc22
                                    2004008210

Printed in the USA

CG/CG

table of contents

Mambas

The mamba is a close cousin of the cobra, shown here—a cobra without a hood.

The Jameson's mamba, the black mamba, and the two **species** of green mamba are members of the *Elapidae* family. Like all snakes, mambas are **reptiles**.

Many people are more afraid of the African mamba than they are of any other snake because of its **venom**. The black mamba can move with its head and front part of its body above the ground.

Africans fear the black mamba not only for its bite but also for its great speed.

4

Where They Live

Green mambas live in the trees and bushes of the African **savannah**. Green mambas live in trees and glide through their branches. The Jameson's mamba lives in the trees of central Africa. The black mamba lives among rocks, in tall grasses, and on the forest floor.

A black mamba coils under a favorite hiding place, an old stump.

The East African green mamba is a skilled climber.

Did you know?

Mambas can travel at speeds of up to 7 miles (11 kilometers) an hour.

Did you know?

The green mamba is 6 to 7 feet (about 2 meters) long. The black mamba can grow to 14 feet (4.3 m) long.

What they look like

Mambas have slim, muscular bodies covered with smooth scales. Green mambas are green, yellow, and black. The West African green mamba has large green scales bordered by black. Black mambas are actually brown or gray.

Raindrops gather on the scales of an East African green mamba.

The West African mamba can be easily identified by its large scales.

their senses

The mambas' eyesight and sense of smell are better than those of many snakes. Their large eyes see **prey** better than do most snakes. The **Jacobson's organ** in the roof of the snake's mouth analyzes particles brought to it by the snake's tongue. Then the mamba follows prey for the kill.

A black mamba flicks its forked tongue to learn more about the things around it.

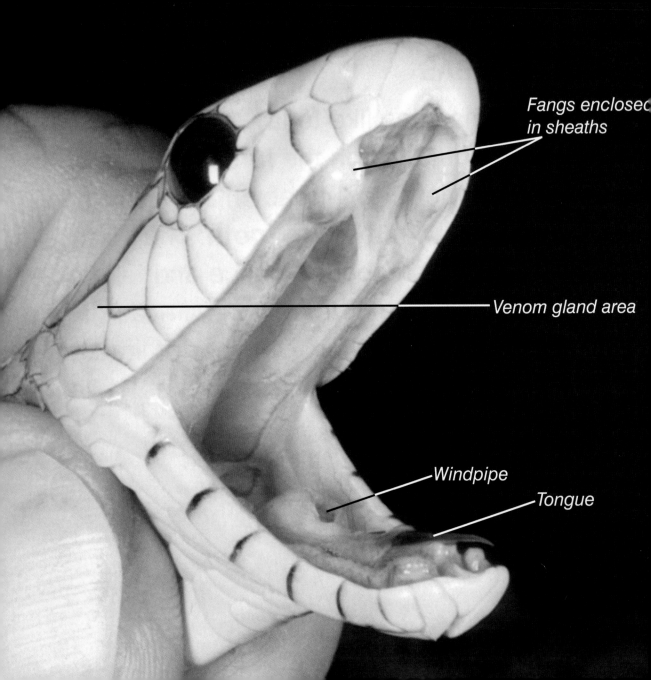

Fangs enclosed
in sheaths

Venom gland area

Windpipe

Tongue

the Head and Mouth

The mamba has a tapered snout. This allows the snake to see objects fairly well. There are hollow fangs at the front of the upper jaw.

When the snake strikes, venom in the venom glands is pumped through the fangs and into the prey.

A green mamba's head shows its large eyes and other features.

The snake's jaws stretch so the snake can swallow whole animals. The windpipe runs from the throat to the front of the mouth. This lets the snake breathe while it is swallowing.

A West African green mamba dines on a small animal.

Baby Mambas

Female mambas lay their eggs in damp growth on the forest floor. In spring or early summer 9 to 14 babies hatch from the eggs. The babies are 15 to 24 inches (38 to 61 centimeters) long. They weigh about an ounce when they are born and can take care of themselves right away.

A baby mamba glides past its recently shed skin.

A baby black mamba is already equipped with fangs and venom.

Did you know?

Black mambas grow 4-1/2 feet (1.4 m) in their first year.

their Prey

Mambas eat rats, rice, squirrels, and birds. The green mamba watches for prey to move within striking distance. The mamba's strike reaches almost half its body length. The mamba bites the prey's neck and rarely releases it.

An East African green mamba hangs on a tree limb to catch birds.

Did you know?

Because the green mamba lives in trees, it cannot let its prey fall to the ground.

their Defense

The green mamba is **camouflaged** from most enemies by leaves and branches. Black mambas hide in tree stumps, rocks, and burrows. If the mamba feels threatened by an enemy, the snake will bite the attacker.

A mamba's strike can reach half its body length.

Green coloring helps this mamba camouflage itself in leaves.

Mambas and People

Experts think that just two drops of the black mamba's venom can kill a human. Only those who get treatment immediately are able to survive. Mambas are shy and will try to stay away from humans.

Scientists think that studying the mamba's venom may be useful in helping to understand the secrets of the human brain.

Glossary

camouflaged (KAM uh flahzd) — disguised by fitting in with the creature's background

Jacobson's organ (JAYK ub sunz ORG un) — the part of a snake that analyzes a scent the snake has picked up

prey (PRAY) — animals hunted and killed by other animals for food

reptiles (REP TYLZ) — animals with cold blood, a backbone, and scales or plates

savannah (suh VAN uh) — tropical grasslands with some tree growth

species (SPEE sheez) — a certain kind of plant or animal within a closely related group

venom (VEN um) — poisonous substance contained in many snakes

index

Further Reading

Richardson, Adele D. *Mambas*. Capstone, 2003
"Mamba." *International Wildlife Encyclopedia, vol. 11.* Cavendish, 2002
Solway, Andrew. *Deadly Snakes.* Heinemann Library, 2004

Websites to Visit

animal.discovery.com/fansites/jeffcorwin/carnival/slithering/blackmamba.html
www.enchantedlearning.com/subjects/reptiles/snakes/printouts.shtml
www.nwf.org/internationalwildlife/mamba.html

About the Author

Ted O'Hare is an author and editor of children's nonfiction books. He divides his time between New York City and a home upstate.